GW00632142

# SONIA ALLISON'S
# SWEETS BOOK

Also by Sonia Allison in this series:
SONIA ALLISON'S BISCUIT BOOK
SONIA ALLISON'S BREAD BOOK

# SONIA ALLISON'S
# SWEETS BOOK

PIATKUS

© 1983 Sonia Allison

First published in 1983 by Judy Piatkus (Publishers) Limited
of Loughton, Essex

British Library Cataloguing in Publication Data

Allison, Sonia
  Sonia Allison's sweets book
  1. **Confectionery**
  I. Title
  641.8'53      TX 791

ISBN 0-86188-167-2


Designed by Paul Saunders
Cover designed by Ken Leeder

Typeset by Gilbert Composing Services, Leighton Buzzard
Printed and bound by The Pitman Press, Bath

# CONTENTS

# INTRODUCTION

Sweets are for everyone, and when homemade with a sprinkling of love and the best things of life, what could be better! Smooth, golden fudge, or a rich coffee version studded with nuts; crackling, buttery butterscotch; exotic Turkish Delight; mellow, Continental-style truffles laced with alcohol; expensive-tasting marzipan fruits of many colours packed with real almonds; mint creams brushed with the darkest of plain chocolate; old fashioned Brazil nut toffee; genuine, sticky honeycomb; coconut ice; petit fours – all these and more besides add up to a mouth-watering assortment of do-it-yourself sweets for family enjoyment, year-round gifts for special friends, bazaars, fêtes, bring and buy sales and, indeed, any other occasion where a box of one's own efforts is welcomed and appreciated with genuine pleasure.

# Hints and Tips

1. Some sweets are easier to make than others and require minimal cooking. Others need longer over heat and can become very hot indeed. May I, therefore, ask you please to keep children and animals away from the cooking area in case of accidents.

2. Choose a strong, heavy-based saucepan for boiling toffees and fudges, etc., and make sure it is also reasonably deep. This is because these mixtures tend to rise up in the pan and can easily boil over if the pan is shallow.

3. Always stir with a wooden handled spoon or wooden stick. NEVER use metal as the handle gets unpleasantly hot and can burn the hand.

4. Make sure that tins into which cooked sweet mixtures will be poured or spread are greased with butter or margarine BEFORE YOU START. Very often a mixture will set quickly once it has reached the correct temperature and if it is then left while you get the tin ready, it may become unmanageable and unspreadable.

**5.** Any sweets containing eggs, butter and cream should be eaten within a week and refrigerated after three days. Truffles can be deep frozen successfully for up to about six weeks.

**6.** Apart from toffees and caramels, which need to be individually wrapped (I use film or colourless cellophane), all sweets look better if placed in paper sweet cases which are available from stationers, some kitchen boutiques and gift shops.

**7.** Assorted sweets, intended for gifts, should be prettily packed and tastefully boxed, and here imaginative flair and creative talents play their own rôle as one selects wrappings, ribbons and stickers for decoration.

# Testing for Setting

Once upon a time, sweet-making enthusiasts invested in a sugar thermometer which went way beyond blood heat and registered the correct temperature for each type of sweet; for instance, toffee needs a higher temperature than fudge if it is going to set properly. Given that a thermometer of this kind is no longer a part of the average kitchen, here are alternative ways of testing.

Pour a little of the mixture into a cup of cold water and then test as follows:

### For Fudge
Mixture should form a ball which flattens between finger and thumb.

### For Caramels and Soft Toffees
Mixture should form a firm ball with a pliable texture.

### For Brittles, Hard Toffees and Butterscotch
Mixture should form threads which are brittle and snap easily.

# TRUFFLES

Based primarily on chocolate, truffles are a calculated plot against all those counting calories and prove that the best things in life are rich, fattening, seductive and luxurious! Requiring the minimal amount of cooking, truffles make fabulous presents for chocolate addicts. To give them a chic and authentic look, so characteristic of their French counterparts, roll them into slightly irregular-shaped balls, then coat them liberally with drinking chocolate or cocoa powder. No self-respecting truffle is enamoured with chocolate vermicelli (which all falls off anyway if you are not careful), so I've kept the coatings plain, the truffles assorted.

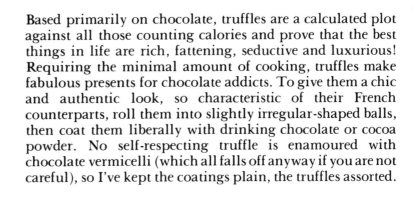

# Milk Chocolate Truffles

**Makes 12**

*4 oz (125 g) milk chocolate*
*1 oz (25 g) butter*
*½ tsp vanilla essence*
*2 oz (50 g) icing sugar, sifted*
*Drinking chocolate or*
*    cocoa powder*

These truffles, and the ones that follow, are similar to the expensive handmade kind found in confectionary shops abroad, and sometimes here as well.

**1.** Break up chocolate and put, with butter, into a basin standing over a pan of hot water. Leave until melted, stirring once or twice.

**2.** Mix in vanilla essence and icing sugar. Set aside for about 15 minutes or until mixture firms up (but do not leave in the refrigerator).

**3.** Roll into 12 irregular-shaped balls, then coat with drinking chocolate or cocoa, sifted on to a piece of foil.

**4.** Put into paper cases and store in an airtight container. Keep in the cool.

*Makes 12*             **Dark Chocolate Truffles**
                       Make exactly as Milk Chocolate Truffles but use plain dessert
                       chocolate instead of milk.

*Makes 12*             **Rum Truffles**
                       Make up Milk or Dark Chocolate Truffles but use rum essence
                       instead of vanilla.

*Makes 12*             **Sherry Truffles**
                       Make up Milk or Dark Chocolate Truffles but use sherry essence
                       instead of vanilla.

# French-style Truffles

*Makes 20*

4 oz (125 g) plain dessert
  chocolate
2 oz (50 g) butter, at kitchen
  temperature and soft
3 oz (75 g) icing sugar, sifted
2 egg yolks from Grade 2
  eggs
½ tsp vanilla essence
Drinking chocolate or
  cocoa powder

Soft, smooth and exclusive, these are the sort of truffles that cost the
earth to buy, yet are within the bounds of financial reality when
homemade.

1. Break up chocolate and put into a basin standing over a pan of
hot water. Leave until melted, stirring once or twice.

2. Put butter into a bowl. Add sugar. Cream until light and fluffy.

3. Stir in egg yolks, vanilla essence and melted chocolate.

4. Allow to cool then refrigerate until firm enough to handle.

5. Roll into 20 irregular-shaped balls, then coat with drinking
chocolate or cocoa, sifted on to a piece of foil.

6. Put into paper cases and store in an airtight container. Keep in
the cool.

14

| | |
|---|---|
| *Makes 20* | **French-style Coffee Truffles**<br>Make exactly as French-style Truffles, but instead of vanilla essence add 1 heaped teaspoon instant coffee powder dissolved in 1 to 1½ teaspoons boiling water. |
| *Makes 20* | **French-style Orange Truffles**<br>Make exactly as French-style Truffles, but instead of vanilla essence add 1 level teaspoon very finely grated orange peel. |

# Whisky Nut Truffles

***Makes 16***

6 oz (175 g) plain dessert
    chocolate
1 oz (25 g) butter, at kitchen
    temperature and soft
1 Grade 3 egg yolk
1 oz (25 g) walnuts, finely
    chopped
3 tsp whisky
Drinking chocolate or
    cocoa powder

Expensive-tasting, luscious truffles which are quickly made by beating all the ingredients together.

**1.** Break up chocolate and put into a basin standing over a pan of hot water. Leave until melted, stirring once or twice.

**2.** Remove basin from saucepan, then add butter, egg yolk, walnuts and whisky.

**3.** Beat for 2 to 3 minutes or until thoroughly mixed.

**4.** Leave in the refrigerator to firm-up slightly (but not for too long or mixture will harden), then roll into 16 irregular-shaped balls.

**5.** Coat with drinking chocolate or cocoa, sifted on to a piece of foil.

**6.** Put into paper cases and store in an airtight container. Keep in the cool.

*Makes 16*

**Rum Nut Truffles**
Make exactly as Whisky Nut Truffles but substitute dark rum for the whisky.

*Makes 16*

**Sherry Nut Truffles**
Make exactly as Whisky Nut Truffles but substitute sweet cream sherry for the whisky.

*Makes 16*

**Grand Marnier Nut Truffles**
Make exactly as Whisky Nut Truffles but substitute Grand Marnier for the whisky.

# Black Forest Cherry Truffles

*Makes 24*

*4 oz (125 g) plain dessert chocolate*
*2 oz (50 g) butter, melted*
*2 Grade 3 egg yolks, at room temperature*
*2 tblsp cherry brandy*
*2 oz (50 g) ground almonds*
*6 oz (175 g) icing sugar, sifted*
*Drinking chocolate or cocoa powder*

*Makes 24*

1. Break up chocolate and put into a basin standing over a pan of hot water. Leave until melted, stirring once or twice.

2. Mix in butter, egg yolks, cherry brandy and almonds.

3. Gradually work in icing sugar.

4. Spread into a dish or on to a plate and leave in a cool place for ¾ to 1 hour, or until firm enough to handle.

5. Roll into 24 irregular-shaped balls, then coat with drinking chocolate or cocoa, sifted on to a piece of foil.

6. Put into paper cases and store in an airtight container. Keep in the cool.

## Coffee Liqueur Truffles
Make exactly as Black Forest Cherry Truffles but use Tia Maria instead of cherry brandy.

# Cream Cheese Chocolate Truffles

**Makes 24**

4 oz (125 g) plain dessert
chocolate
½ oz (15 g) butter
2 tsp warm water
3 oz (75 g) cream cheese, at
  kitchen temperature
1 tsp vanilla essence
6 oz (175 g) icing sugar,
  sifted
Drinking chocolate or
  cocoa powder

1. Break up chocolate and put, with butter, into a basin standing over a pan of hot water. Leave until melted, stirring once or twice.

2. Put cream cheese into a bowl and beat until smooth.

3. Gradually beat in vanilla essence, melted chocolate and butter, and finally the icing sugar.

4. When thoroughly mixed, put on to a plate and refrigerate until firm enough to handle.

5. Roll into 24 irregular-shaped balls and coat with drinking chocolate or cocoa, sifted on to a piece of foil.

6. Put into paper cases and store in an airtight container. Keep in the cool.

# Cake Crumb Chocolate Truffles

***Makes 30 to 34***

*4 oz (125 g) plain dessert chocolate*
*2 oz (50 g) butter*
*1 Grade 3 egg yolk, at kitchen temperature*
*4 oz (125 g) icing sugar, sifted*
*4 oz (125 g) cake crumbs*
*2 tblsp rum or sweet cream sherry*
*Drinking chocolate or cocoa powder*

***Makes 30 to 34***

Not too expensive, and more long-lasting than those made with cream, these Cake Crumb Truffles may be made about two weeks before Christmas and given away as gifts.

**1.** Break up chocolate and put, with butter, into a basin standing over a pan of hot water. Leave until melted, stirring once or twice.

**2.** Remove basin from pan then stir in egg yolk, icing sugar, cake crumbs and rum or sherry. Mix thoroughly.

**3.** Leave in the cool for 10 minutes or until firm but pliable.

**4.** Roll into 30 to 34 balls, then coat with drinking chocolate or cocoa, sifted on to a piece of foil.

**5.** Put into paper cases and store in an airtight container.

### Almond and Cake Crumb Chocolate Truffles
Make exactly as Cake Crumb Chocolate Truffles but use half cake crumbs and half ground almonds.

20

# Cream Truffles

**Makes 18**

2 oz (50 g) plain chocolate
2 tblsp double cream
1 tsp vanilla essence
8 oz (225 g) icing sugar,
    sifted
Drinking chocolate or
    cocoa powder

Reasonably economical despite the cream, these truffles use a small amount of chocolate and a highish proportion of icing sugar.

1. Break up chocolate and melt in a basin standing over a pan of hot water.

2. Stir in cream, vanilla essence and icing sugar.

3. Spread out on to a plate and leave in the cool until mixture firms up slightly.

4. Roll into 18 irregular-shaped balls and coat with drinking chocolate or cocoa, sifted on to a piece of foil.

5. Put into paper cases and store in an airtight container. Keep in the cool.

21

# Economy Truffles

***Makes 15***

*2 oz (50 g) butter, at kitchen
     temperature and soft*
*2 oz (50 g) caster sugar*
*½ tsp vanilla essence*
*3 oz (75 g) Madeira cake
     crumbs*
*2 rounded tsp cocoa
     powder, sifted*
*2 rounded tsp plum jam, at
     kitchen temperature*
*Drinking chocolate or
     cocoa powder*

An economical truffle recipe, useful when you have a little leftover Madeira cake.

1. Cream butter, sugar and essence together until light and fluffy.

2. Stir in cake crumbs, cocoa powder and jam. Mix thoroughly.

3. If too soft to handle, refrigerate until mixture firms up.

4. Roll into 15 balls and coat with drinking chocolate or cocoa, sifted on to a piece of foil.

# FONDANTS

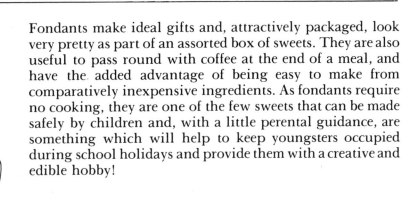

Fondants make ideal gifts and, attractively packaged, look very pretty as part of an assorted box of sweets. They are also useful to pass round with coffee at the end of a meal, and have the added advantage of being easy to make from comparatively inexpensive ingredients. As fondants require no cooking, they are one of the few sweets that can be made safely by children and, with a little perental guidance, are something which will help to keep youngsters occupied during school holidays and provide them with a creative and edible hobby!

# Peppermint Creams

***Makes just over 1 lb or 450 g***

1 Grade 2 egg white
1 tsp peppermint essence
1 lb (450 g) icing sugar,
    sifted
2 tsp glycerine (to prevent
    fondants from hardening
    up too much)

A favourite with everybody, especially when served as petit fours.

1. Beat egg white until it just begins to look frothy.

2. Add peppermint essence and sufficient sugar to form a stiff paste.

3. If you find the mixture too stiff, add 1 or 2 teaspoons water; if too soft, work in a little extra sifted icing sugar.

4. Turn out on to a work top sprinkled with plenty of sifted icing sugar and knead lightly until smooth.

5. Roll out to about ¼-inch (just under 1 cm) thickness, then cut into rounds with a 1-inch (2½ cm) plain or fluted biscuit cutter, re-rolling and re-cutting trimmings into more rounds.

*Makes just over 1 lb or 450 g*   **Sherwood Creams**
Make exactly as Peppermint Creams but tint mixture pale green
with food colouring.

*Makes just over 1 lb or 450 g*   **Chocolate Peppermint Creams**
Using an artist's paint-brush, brush designs on top of Peppermint
Creams (or Sherwood Creams) with melted plain dessert chocolate.

# Rose Creams

*Makes 1 lb 2 oz or 500 g*

1 lb (450 g) icing sugar
2 oz (50 g) butter
2 tblsp double cream
1 tsp rose essence
Few drops rose pink
   colouring
Crystallised rose petals to
   decorate

1. Sift icing sugar into a bowl.

2. Put the butter and double cream into a saucepan. Melt over a very low heat, taking care not to let the mixture boil.

3. Stir in rose essence. Very gradually add to the icing sugar.

4. Mix to a paste, then work in colouring. Turn out on to a board dusted with extra sifted icing sugar and knead until smooth.

5. Shape into about 30 round balls, drop into paper cases and put a crystallised rose petal on top of each. Leave to harden before eating. Store in an airtight tin.

*Makes 1 lb 3 oz or 525 g*

## Coconut Cherry Creams
Make exactly as Rose Creams but add 1 oz (25 g) desiccated coconut to the icing sugar. Omit rose essence and flavour with vanilla essence instead. Tint pale pink with red food colouring. Roll into about 30 balls and drop into paper cases. Top each with half a glacé cherry.

**Makes 1 lb 2 oz or 500 g**

### Lemon Kisses

Make exactly as Rose Creams, but omit rose essence and flavour mixture with lemon essence. Tint pale lemon with yellow food colouring. Shape into about 30 round balls, drop into paper cases and put a hazelnut on top of each. Leave to harden before eating. Store in an airtight tin.

**Makes 1 lb 2 oz or 500 g**

### Orange Diamonds

Make exactly as Rose Creams, but omit rose essence and flavour mixture with orange essence. Tint pale orange with food colouring. After kneading, roll out to ¼-inch (just under 1 cm) thickness and cut into diamond shapes. Press a piece of walnut on top of each. Store in an airtight tin.

**Makes 1 lb 2 oz or 500 g**

### Coffee Flutes

Make exactly as Rose Creams, but omit rose essence and add 2 rounded teaspoons instant coffee powder when melting butter and cream. After kneading, roll out to ¼-inch (just under 1 cm) thickness and cut into 1-inch (2½ cm) rounds with a fluted biscuit cutter. Press a hazelnut on top of each and leave to harden before eating. Store in an airtight tin.

*Makes 1 lb 2 oz or 500 g*

## Raspberry Half Moons

Make exactly as Rose Creams, but omit rose essence and flavo
mixture with raspberry essence. Tint pale pink with red foo
colouring. After kneading, roll out to ¼-inch (just under 1 cr
thickness. Cut into rounds with a 1-inch (2½ cm) fluted biscu
cutter, then cut each round in half to make half moons. If like
brush half with melted chocolate and leave the other half plai

*Makes 1 lb 4 oz or 550 g*

## Nutty Butterscotch Creams

Make exactly as Rose Creams, but add 2 oz (50 g) very fine
chopped walnuts to the icing sugar. Omit rose essence and flavo
with butterscotch essence instead. Either leave plain or tint golde
brown with a little gravy browning or brown food colouring. Ro
out to ¼-inch (just under 1 cm) thickness and roll into about 30 lo
shapes. Leave to harden before eating. Store in an airtight tin.

# MARZIPAN SWEETS

Marzipan is like adult plasticine and, because it is so easy to mould, is marvellous for making an assortment of miniature fruits, vegetables and other novelty sweets, such as Marzipan Walnuts, Cherries and Prunes, which are so useful for petit fours and gift giving. There is one basic recipe and very attractive effects can be achieved by using food colouring. Marzipan also has good staying powers and can be stored for up to two months in an airtight tin.

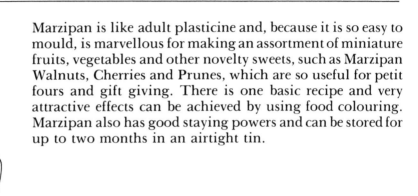

29

# Marzipan

***Makes just over 1 lb or 450 g***

*4 oz (125 g) icing sugar*
*4 oz (125 g) caster sugar*
*8 oz (225 g) ground*
  *almonds*
*1 tsp almond essence*
*½ tsp vanilla essence*
*1 Grade 3 egg, lightly*
  *beaten*
*Lemon juice*

This is the basic recipe from which many attractive sweets can be created.

1. Sift icing sugar into a bowl. Toss in caster sugar and ground almonds.

2. Mix to a STIFF paste with essences and egg, adding 1 or 2 teaspoons lemon juice if mixture stays on the dry and crumbly side.

3. Turn out on to a surface sprinkled lightly with sugar and knead until smooth. Divide into 6 equal portions and follow any of the recipe variations that follow for fruits, vegetables and fancies.

# Marzipan Fruits

### Marzipan Oranges
Take 1 portion of marzipan and knead in some orange food colouring. Roll into small round balls and press against the sides of a grater to give the impression of genuine orange skin. Put into paper sweet cases.

### Marzipan Lemons
Take 1 portion of marzipan and knead in some yellow food colouring. Form into small lemon shapes, then continue as for the Marzipan Oranges.

### Marzipan Bananas
Take 1 portion of marzipan and knead in some yellow food colouring. Shape into small bananas, then mark in brown streaks with an artist's paint-brush dipped in gravy browning. Put into paper cases.

### Marzipan Apples
Take 1 portion of marzipan and knead in some green food colouring. Shape into small balls and put a clove into the top of each to represent the stalk. Add 'blushes' of red by applying red food colouring with an artist's paint-brush. Put into paper cases.

### Marzipan Pears
Take 1 portion of marzipan and knead in some green food colouring. Shape into small pears and continue as for apples.

### Marzipan Strawberries
Take 1 portion of marzipan and knead in some red food colouring. Shape into small strawberries, then 'stipple' all over with a fork. Put a clove into the top of each to represent the stalk.

# Marzipan Vegetables

Make up half quantity of marzipan as previously directed and divide into 3 equal portions.

### Marzipan Carrots
Take 1 portion of marzipan and knead in some orange food colouring. Shape into small carrots and put a clove in the top of each to represent the stalk. Put into paper cases.

### Marzipan Potatoes
Take 1 portion of marzipan, roll into irregular-shaped potatoes and toss in cocoa powder. Put into paper cases.

### Marzipan Cauliflowers
Take 1 portion of marzipan and divide in half. Colour 1 half green with food colouring. Shape remainder into small balls and 'stipple' tops with a fork. Cover outside with green 'leaves', shaped from second half of marzipan.

# Marzipan Fancies

Make up marzipan as previously directed then divide into
portions and use as follows:

**Marzipan Walnuts**
Sandwich walnut halves together with plain or pink-coloured
marzipan. Put into paper cases.

**Marzipan Dates**
Stone dessert dates and fill with marzipan. Put into paper cases.

**Marzipan Cherries**
Pack hazelnuts into glacé cherries, then wrap each in marzipan.
Put into paper cases.

**Marzipan Gingers**
Roll marzipan into smallish balls and drop into paper cases. Top
each with a thick slice of preserved ginger.

## Marzipan Pinwheels

Halve marzipan and colour 1 portion deep pink. On a sugared surface, roll both pieces out into equal-sized squares. Put one on top of the other then roll up like a Swiss roll. Cut into thinnish slices. Serve on a sugar-coated fancy plate.

## Marzipan Prunes

Stone plump prunes, then fill with marzipan.

# FUDGE

Love it dearly though I do, I have to admit that fudge has a will of its own and, even if one makes up the same recipe a hundred times, the results can vary from batch to batch. One can end up with some fudge which is softer than others, some which is crisper and approaching the sort of crumbly texture associated with old-fashioned cough candy, and some which is as smooth as fondant and almost more creamy than it should be. Much depends, of course, on how long the mixture has been allowed to boil. If underdone, fudge simply will not fudge to a cutable consistency, and my alternative, under those circumstances, is to roll it into plumpish marbles, drop them into paper cases and decorate them as the mood takes me - with nuts, pieces of glacé fruits, little pieces of date or, if to be eaten within hours, crystallised flower petals such as violet or rose. They become a sort of mystery sweet, beloved by all with a proverbial sweet tooth. The eleven variations I give in the first recipe, Buttery Vanilla Fudge, can be used as variations in most of the cooked varieties.

The fudges in the first part of this section are all cooked ones, and then follow easier varieties which require minimal attention and no boiling - a bonus for those who are anxious about getting the temperature right, worried in case the consistency is wrong and a bit concerned about the work involved in fudge making.

# Buttery Vanilla Fudge

**Makes about 2 lb or 900 g**

½ pt (275 ml) milk
1¾ lb (800 g) granulated
  sugar
4 oz (125 g) butter
2 tsp vanilla essence

This works well - or has done for me for many years - and takes kindly to additions.

1. Well grease a 7-inch (17½ cm) square tin or small roasting tin.

2. Put milk, sugar and butter into a saucepan.

3. Heat slowly, stirring all the time, until sugar dissolves.

4. Bring to boil, still stirring. Cover. Boil slowly for 2 minutes. Uncover.

5. Continue to boil, uncovered, over a medium heat for about 15 to 20 minutes or until a little of the mixture forms a softish ball when dropped into a cup of really cold water. At this point you should be able to roll the ball between finger and thumb without it disintegrating. Stir often to prevent sticking.

**6.** Remove from heat and either leave to stand for 15 minutes or place the saucepan in a sink containing about 4 inches (10 cm) very cold water.

**7.** Add vanilla essence and beat fudge until it loses its gloss and starts to thicken. Spread into tin with knife.

**8.** Mark into squares, then cut up when set – something which should happen fairly quickly. Store in an airtight tin.

*Makes about 2 lb or 900 g*

**Buttery Coffee Fudge**
Make as Buttery Vanilla Fudge, but add 2 tablespoons coffee essence drink (such as Camp) to the pan with all the other ingredients. Omit vanilla.

*Makes about 2¼ lb or 1 kg*

**Buttery Fruit and Nut Fudge**
Make as Buttery Vanilla Fudge but add 2 oz (50 g) sultanas or raisins and 1½ oz (40 g) coarsely chopped almonds to fudge just before beating.

*Makes just over 2 lb or 900 g*

**Buttery Coconut Fudge**
Make as Buttery Vanilla Fudge but add 1½ oz (40 g) desiccated coconut to fudge just before beating.

*Makes about 2¼ lb or 1 kg*

**Buttery Toasted Almond Fudge**
Make as Buttery Vanilla Fudge but add 4 oz (125 g) lightly toasted flaked almonds and 2 teaspoons almond essence to fudge just before beating.

*Makes just over 2 lb or 900 g*

**Buttery Coffee Nut Fudge**
Make as Buttery Coffee Fudge (page 39) but add 2 oz (50 g) chopped walnuts to fudge just before beating.

*Makes about 2 lb or 900 g*

**Buttery Cocoa Fudge**
Make as Buttery Vanilla Fudge but add 3 level tablespoons cocoa powder with the other main ingredients.

*Makes about 2¼ lb or 1 kg*    **Buttery Chocolate Fudge**
Make as Buttery Vanilla Fudge, but add 1 bar (3½ oz or 100g) plain chocolate, broken up into squares, to the pan with the other main ingredients.

*Makes about 2 lb or 900 g*    **Buttery Rum or Sherry Fudge**
Make as Buttery Vanilla Fudge but use rum or sherry essence instead of vanilla.

*Makes about 2 lb or 900 g*    **Buttery Mint Fudge**
Make as Buttery Vanilla Fudge, but use 1 teaspoon peppermint essence instead of vanilla.

*Makes about 2 lb or 900 g*    **Buttery Orange Fudge**
Make as Buttery Vanilla Fudge but add 1 teaspoon orange essence instead of vanilla.

*Makes about 2 lb or 900 g*    **Buttery Raspberry Fudge**
Make as Buttery Vanilla Fudge but add 1 teaspoon raspberry essence instead of vanilla.

# Condensed Milk Fudge

***Makes 2 lb or 900 g***

*1½ lb (675 g) granulated
  sugar*
*¼ pt (150 ml) water*
*1 large can sweetened
  condensed milk*
*2 oz (50 g) butter*
*2 tsp vanilla essence*

A warm, golden-coloured fudge with a lovely flavour.

**1.** Well grease a 7-inch (17½ cm) square tin or small roasting tin.

**2.** Put sugar, water, milk and butter into a pan and stir over a low heat until sugar dissolves.

**3.** Bring to boil over medium heat. Cover. Boil for 2 minutes. Uncover.

**4.** Continue to boil, uncovered, for about 20 minutes or until a little of the mixture, dropped into a cup of very cold water, forms a softish ball. At this point you should be able to roll the ball between finger and thumb without it disintegrating.

**5.** Stir often to prevent sticking, then, when fudge is ready, draw pan away from heat and either leave to stand for 15 minutes or place the saucepan in a sink containing about 4 inches (10 cm) very cold water.

**6.** Add vanilla essence and beat fudge until it loses its gloss and starts to thicken. Spread into tin with knife.

**7.** Mark into squares, then cut up when set – something which should happen fairly quickly. Store in an airtight tin.

**Variations**
As Buttery Vanilla Fudge.

# Evaporated Milk Fudge

*Makes about 1 lb or 450 g*

*1 small can (6 oz or 175 g)*
  *evaporated milk*
  *(unsweetened)*
*1 lb (450 g) granulated*
  *sugar*
*2 oz (50 g) butter*
*1 tsp vanilla essence*

Make exactly as Condensed Milk Fudge, adding ingredients to pan in the order listed.

**Variations**
As Buttery Vanilla Fudge.

# Honey Fudge

***Makes about 1 lb or 450 g***

1 lb (450 g) granulated
   sugar
4 rounded tblsp thick
   honey
1 small can (6 oz or 175 g)
   evaporated milk
   (unsweetened)
2 oz (50 g) butter
1 tsp vanilla essence

A distinctively flavoured fudge, due to the inclusion of honey instead of syrup.

Make exactly as Condensed Milk Fudge (pages 42–43), adding ingredients to pan in the order listed.

**Variations**
As Buttery Vanilla Fudge.

# Golden Syrup Fudge

*Makes about 1 lb or 450 g*

2 oz (50 g) golden syrup
1 lb (450 g) granulated
   sugar
2 oz (50 g) butter
¼ pt (150 ml) single cream
1 tsp vanilla essence

Make exactly as Condensed Milk Fudge (pages 42–43), adding ingredients to pan in the order listed, but cook a little longer so that a small amount of mixture, dropped into a cup of cold water, forms a firmish ball as opposed to a soft one.

**Variations**
As Buttery Vanilla Fudge.

**Tip**
If Fudge stays on the soft side, roll into marbles, drop into paper cases and decorate to taste. They will firm up in the refrigerator but soften again at room temperature. They make excellent petit fours with coffee.

# Marshmallow Fudge

**Makes about 1¼ lb or 575 g**

1 lb (450 g) granulated
   sugar
¼ pt (150 ml) milk
2 oz (50 g) butter
1 level tblsp golden syrup
4 oz (125 g) marshmallows

1. Well grease a 7-inch (17½ cm) square tin or small roasting tin.

2. Put sugar, milk, butter and syrup into a saucepan.

3. Heat slowly, stirring all the time, until sugar dissolves.

4. Bring to the boil, cover and cook for 1 minute. Uncover.

5. Continue to boil for 5 to 10 minutes (length of time will depend on the depth of pan – the deeper it is, the longer the mixture will take) when a little of the mixture, dropped into a cup of cold water, should form a softish ball.

6. Reduce heat, add marshmallows and stir until melted.

7. Boil for a further 2 minutes, remove pan from heat and cool for 7 minutes.

8. Beat hard for about 5 to 8 minutes or until fudge loses its gloss and thickens. Spread into tin. Mark into squares. Cut up when cold. Store in an airtight tin.

*Makes 1¼ lb or 575 g*

**Marshmallow Coffee Fudge**
Make as Marshmallow Fudge but add 2 rounded teaspoons instant coffee powder with the marshmallows.

*Makes 1¼ lb or 575 g*

**Marshmallow Peppermint Fudge**
Make as Marshmallow Fudge but add 1 teaspoon peppermint essence with the marshmallows.

*Makes 1¼ lb or 575 g*

**Marshmallow Lemon Fudge**
Make as Marshmallow Fudge but add 1 teaspoon lemon essence with the marshmallows.

*Makes 1¼ lb or 575 g*

**Marshmallow Almond Fudge**
Make as Marshmallow Fudge but add ½ teaspoon almond essence with the marshmallows.

*Makes 1¼ lb or 575 g*

**Marshmallow Banana Fudge**
Make as Marshmallow Fudge but add ½ teaspoon banana essence with the marshmallows.

# Treacle Fudge

*Makes about 1 lb (450 g)*

This fudge is dark, rich and delicious.

1 lb (450 g) granulated
  sugar
4 level tblsp black treacle
6 tblsp milk
2 oz (50 g) butter

Make exactly as Condensed Milk Fudge, adding ingredients to
pan in order listed.

*Makes 1 lb 2 oz or 500 g*

**Treacle and Peanut Fudge**
Make as Treacle Fudge but add 2 oz (50 g) chopped peanuts after
other ingredients.

*Makes 1 lb 2 oz or 500 g*

**Treacle Walnut Fudge**
Make as Treacle Fudge but add 2 oz (50 g) chopped walnuts after
other ingredients.

# Coffee Hazelnut Fudge

**Makes about 1½ lb or 675 g**

2 oz (50 g) hazelnuts
3 oz (75 g) butter
3 tblsp coffee essence drink
2 tblsp evaporated
    (unsweetened) or long-
    life milk
1 lb (450 g) icing sugar,
    sieved

A minimal-cook version which is made with total ease. There is also something very Continental – and special – about the combination of coffee and hazelnuts.

1. Line a shallow tin measuring 11 by 7 inches (27½ by 17½ cm) with non-stick Bakewell parchment paper.

2. Coarsely chop hazelnuts and leave on one side for the time being.

3. Put butter and coffee essence into a pan and melt over a low heat. Draw aside.

4. Add evaporated or long-life milk, chopped nuts and icing sugar.

5. Mix thoroughly, then press into prepared tin. Leave until set, then cut into squares. Store in an airtight tin.

# Chocolate Fast Fudge

***Makes about 1½ lb or 675 g***

*1 bar (3½ oz or 100 g) plain chocolate*
*2 oz (50 g) butter*
*4 tblsp double cream*
*1 tsp vanilla essence*
*1 lb (450 g) icing sugar, sifted*

A beauty of a fudge which is totally unproblematic and fabulous to eat. It is rich and requires no cooking!

1. Line a shallow tin measuring 11 by 7 inches (27½ by 17½ cm) with non-stick Bakewell parchment paper.

2. Break up chocolate and put, with butter, into a basin over hot water. Leave until melted, stirring once or twice.

3. Mix in cream and vanilla essence.

4. Gradually blend in icing sugar.

5. Spread into prepared tin and leave until set.

6. Cut into squares and store in an airtight tin.

***Makes about 1½ lb or 675 g***

**Milk Chocolate Fast Fudge**
Make exactly as Chocolate Fast Fudge but use milk chocolate instead of plain.

*Makes about 1½ lb or 675 g*

**Mocha Fast Fudge**
Make exactly as Chocolate Fast Fudge but use only 2 tablespoons cream plus 2 tablespoons liquid coffee essence.

*Makes about 1 lb 10 oz or 725 g*

**Choc Nut Fast Fudge**
Make exactly as Chocolate Fast Fudge but add 2 oz (50 g) chopped walnuts just before the icing sugar.

*Makes about 1½ lb or 675 g*

**Rum Fast Fudge**
Make exactly as Chocolate Fast Fudge but use only 2 tablespoons cream plus 2 tablespoons rum.

# All-in-One Fruit and Nut Fudge

*Makes about 1½ lb or 675 g*

*1 bar (3½ oz or 100 g)*
*   plain chocolate*
*3 oz (75 g) softened butter or*
*   easy-cream margarine*
*1 lb (450 g) icing sugar*
*1 Grade 4 egg, beaten*
*2 level tblsp sweetened*
*   condensed milk*
*2 oz (50 g) unsalted peanuts,*
*   chopped*
*2 oz (50 g) small raisins*

Using softened butter or soft margarine, melted chocolate and icing sugar, this fudge is another no-cook version which can be made quickly and easily.

**1.** Butter a Swiss roll tin measuring about 11 by 7 inches (27½ by 17½ cm).

**2.** Break up chocolate and put, with butter or margarine, into a basin standing over a pan of hot water. Leave until melted, stirring occasionally.

**3.** Sift icing sugar into a large bowl. Add melted chocolate and margarine, followed by egg, milk, nuts and raisins.

**4.** Beat for about 1 minute until smooth. Spread into prepared tin and leave until set. Cut into squares and store in an airtight tin.

# Coffee Butterscotch Fudge

*Makes about 12 oz or 350 g*

Another minimal-cook fudge based on marshmallows.

*4 oz (125 g) marshmallows*
*2 tblsp whipping cream*
*3 level tsp instant coffee*
  *powder*
*2 oz (50 g) light brown soft*
  *sugar*
*2 oz (50 g) butter*
*4 oz (125 g) icing sugar,*
  *sifted*

1. Butter a small tin or dish, about 6 inches (15 cm) square.

2. Melt marshmallows in 1 tablespoon cream with the powder. Leave aside temporarily.

3. Put rest of cream, sugar and butter into a separate small pan. Heat GENTLY until sugar dissolves. Increase heat and boil briskly for 5 minutes only.

4. Remove from heat and stir in the melted marshmallow mixture and icing sugar.

5. Spread into prepared tin and leave until set. Cut into squares and store in an airtight tin.

# Peppermint Almond Fudge

*Makes about 12 oz or 350 g*

*4 oz (125 g) marshmallows*
*2 tblsp whipping cream*
*1 tsp peppermint essence*
*2 oz (50 g) granulated sugar*
*2 oz (50 g) butter*
*2 oz (50 g) blanched*
  *almonds, cut into strips*
  *and lightly toasted*
*4 oz (125 g) icing sugar,*
  *sifted*
*Green food colouring*

An unusual fudge, tastefully flavoured with almond and peppermint.

1. Butter a small tin or dish, about 6 inches (15 cm) square.

2. Melt marshmallows in 1 tablespoon cream and the peppermint essence. Leave aside temporarily.

3. Put rest of cream, sugar and butter into a separate small pan. Heat GENTLY until sugar dissolves. Increase heat and boil briskly for 5 minutes only.

4. Remove from heat and stir in the melted marshmallows, almonds, icing sugar and a few drops of green food colouring.

5. Spread into prepared tin and leave until set. Cut into squares and store in an airtight tin.

# CARAMELS & TOFFEES

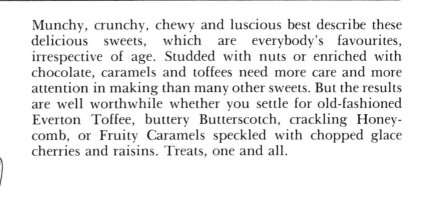

Munchy, crunchy, chewy and luscious best describe these delicious sweets, which are everybody's favourites, irrespective of age. Studded with nuts or enriched with chocolate, caramels and toffees need more care and more attention in making than many other sweets. But the results are well worthwhile whether you settle for old-fashioned Everton Toffee, buttery Butterscotch, crackling Honeycomb, or Fruity Caramels speckled with chopped glace cherries and raisins. Treats, one and all.

55

# Caramels

*Makes about 1¼ lb or 575 g*

4 oz (125 g) butter or
  margarine
2 rounded tblsp golden
  syrup
8 oz (225 g) granulated
  sugar
1 large can sweetened
  condensed milk
1 tsp vanilla essence

1. Butter a 7-inch (17½ cm) shallow square tin.

2. Put all ingredients, except vanilla essence, into a large pan and heat slowly until sugar melts.

3. Bring mixture slowly to the boil, stirring continuously. Cover. Boil gently for 2 minutes. Uncover.

4. Continue to cook steadily, stirring frequently, until mixutre thickens and turns the colour of deep butterscotch. This should take from 15 to 20 minutes.

5. To test for setting, pour a little of the mixture into a cup of cold water. If it forms a firm and pliable ball when rolled between finger and thumb, the caramel is ready.

6. Remove from heat and stir in vanilla essence.

7. Pour into prepared tin and leave for 1½ hours or until half-set.

**8.** Mark into squares and leave for a further 2 to 2½ hours when caramel should be completely set.

**9.** Turn out on to a board and cut into pieces by sawing through with a knife.

**10.** Wrap each piece in a square of cling film or clear cellophane paper.

*Makes about 1½ lb or 675 g* **Nut Caramels**
Make exactly as Caramels but stir in 4 oz (125 g) chopped walnuts or peanuts at the same time as the vanilla essence.

*Makes about 1½ lb or 675 g* **Fruity Caramels**
Make exactly as Caramels but stir in 2 oz (50 g) EACH, chopped glacé cherries and raisins at the same time as the vanilla essence.

*Makes about 1½ lb or 675 g* **Chocolate Caramels**
Make exactly as Caramels but add 1 bar (3½ oz or 100 g) plain dessert chocolate (broken up into squares) with the main ingredients.

# Chocolate Caramels

***Makes about 1¾ lb or 800 g***

2½ oz (65 g) butter
1½ lb (675 g) golden syrup
6 oz (175 g) granulated
  sugar
¼ pt (150 ml) single cream
  or unsweetened
  evaporated milk
1 bar (3½ oz or 100 g) plain
  dessert chocolate, broken
  up into squares
1 tsp vanilla essence

1. Well butter an 8-inch (20 cm) square tin.

2. Put all ingredients into a large pan and bring slowly to boil, stirring continuously. Cover. Boil for 2 minutes. Uncover.

3. Continue to cook and stir over a medium heat for about 20 to 30 minutes or until a little of the mixture, poured into a cup of cold water, forms a firm but pliable ball when rolled between finger and thumb.

4. Pour into prepared tin and mark into squares when half-set (about 1½ hours).

5. Leave for a further 2½ to 3 hours or until caramel is completely set. Turn out on to a board and cut into pieces by sawing through with a knife.

6. Wrap each piece in a square of cling film or clear cellophane paper.

*Makes about 1¾ lb or 800 g*

**Mocha Caramels**
Make as Chocolate Caramels but add 3 rounded teaspoons instant
coffee powder with all the other ingredients.

# Traditional Toffee

*Makes 1¼ lb or 575 g*

*4 rounded tblsp golden
   syrup
1 lb (450 g) granulated
   sugar
2 tsp vinegar
2 tblsp water
2 oz (50 g) butter*

1. Well butter a 7-inch (17½ cm) square tin.

2. Put all ingredients into a saucepan.

3. Heat slowly, stirring, until sugar dissolves. Bring to boil.
Cover. Cook for 2 minutes. Uncover.

4. Continue to boil, without stirring, for a further 7 to 8 minutes or
until a little of the mixture, dropped into a cup of cold water,
separates into threads which are hard and brittle.

5. Pour into prepared tin and leave until hard and set. Break up
into irregular-shaped pieces with a small hammer.

6. Store in an airtight tin.

*Makes 1½ lb or 675 g*

**Traditional Brazil Nut Toffee**
Make exactly as Traditional Toffee but stir 4 oz (125 g) sliced brazil nuts into toffee before pouring into tin.

*Makes 1½ lb or 675 g*

**Traditional Walnut Toffee**
Make exactly as Traditional Toffee but stir 4 oz (125 g) coarsely chopped walnuts into toffee before pouring into tin.

# Butter Honey Toffee

*Makes about 1¼ lb or 575 g*

*1 lb (450 g) light brown soft sugar*
*4 rounded tblsp clear honey*
*6 oz (175 g) butter*
*3 tsp lemon juice*

For those who love the taste of honey, what better treat than this crisp toffee with its warm, deep colour and subtle flavour.

Put all ingredients into a saucepan, then make exactly as directed for Traditional Toffee (page 59).

# Syrup Toffee

**Makes 1¼ lb or 575 g**

*1 lb (450 g) golden syrup*
*4 oz (125 g) butter*
*6 oz (175 g) granulated*
  *sugar*

A sweet golden toffee which is fairly plain but scrumptious to eat. It is also quite easy and quick to make.

Put all ingredients into a saucepan, then make exactly as directed for Traditional Toffee (page 59).

# Treacle Toffee

**Makes about 1 lb or 450 g**

*1 lb (450 g) caster sugar*
*4 level tblsp black treacle or*
  *molasses*
*4 tblsp water*

1. Put all ingredients into a saucepan, then make exactly as directed for Traditional Toffee (page 59), boiling briskly for about 6 to 8 minutes only.

2. To test, pour a little of the mixture into a cup of cold water. If it separates into brittle threads which snap easily, the toffee is ready.

# Everton Toffee

***Makes about 12 oz or 350 g***

*4 tblsp water*
*4 oz (125 g) butter*
*12 oz (350 g) light brown*
*soft sugar*
*2 level tblsp golden syrup*
*1 level tblsp black treacle*

A true oldie, this one, two versions of which appear in my *Cassell's Dictionary of Cooking*, published at the end of the last century.

Put all ingredients into a saucepan, then make exactly as directed for Traditional Toffee (page 59).

# Chocolate Toffee

*Makes 1¼ lb or 575 g*

*oz (125 g) golden syrup*
*tblsp water*
*tsp lemon juice*
*lb (450 g) granulated*
  *sugar*
*oz (50 g) butter*
*bar (3½ oz or 100 g) plain*
  *dessert chocolate*

This has always been the epitome of luxury in toffees as there are few things more enjoyable for the sweet-toothed than a 'chocolate chew'.

Put all ingredients into a saucepan, then make exactly as directed for Traditional Toffee (page 59).

*Makes 1¼ lb or 575 g*

## Chocolate Coffee Toffee
Make as Chocolate Toffee but add 3 rounded teaspoons instant coffee powder with chocolate.

# Coffee Toffee

*Makes about 12 oz or 350 g*

*3 oz (75 g) butter*
*5 oz (150 g) granulated*
*sugar*
*1 level tblsp black treacle*
*2 tblsp coffee essence drink*
*(such as Camp)*
*1 large can sweetened*
*condensed milk*

I am not sure how easy it is to buy coffee-flavoured toffee, so th*i* homemade version should please all coffee devotees.

Put all ingredients into a saucepan, then make exactly as directe* for Traditional Toffee (page 59).

*Makes about 14 oz or 400 g*

**Coffee and Hazelnut Toffee**
Make as Coffee Toffee but add 2 oz (50 g) chopped hazelnuts aft* the other ingredients.

# Toffee Apples

8 medium-sized eating
  apples
8 wooden skewers
¼ pt (150 ml) water
12 oz (350 g) granulated
  sugar
6 oz (175 g) golden syrup
1 tsp vanilla essence
A few drops of red food
  colouring

These are always a treat.

1. Wash and dry apples thoroughly, otherwise toffee will roll off.

2. Push skewers firmly into apples at stalk end.

3. For toffee, put all ingredients into a saucepan, then make exactly as directed for Traditional Toffee (page 59). Colour red with a few drops of food colouring when toffee has finished cooking.

4. Swirl each apple in the toffee then stand on a buttered dish. Leave in the cool until set.

# Condensed Milk Toffee

*Makes 1¼ lb or 575 g*

3 oz (75 g) butter
5 oz (150 g) granulated
  sugar
1 large can sweetened
  condensed milk
1 rounded tblsp golden
  syrup
1 tsp vanilla essence

Put all ingredients into a saucepan, then make exactly as directed
for Traditional Toffee (page 59).

*Makes about 1¼ lb or 575 g*

**Condensed Milk and Cherry Toffee**
Make as Condensed Milk Toffee but add 2 oz (50 g) chopped glacé
cherries after the other ingredients.

*Makes just over 1¼ lb or 575 g*

**Condensed Milk and Walnut Toffee**
Make as Condensed Milk Toffee but add 2 oz (50 g) chopped
walnuts after the other ingredients.

# Butterscotch

*Makes 1 lb or 450 g*

Buttery butterscotch - an old-fashioned sweet.

¼ pt (150 ml) water
1 lb (450 g) light brown soft
   sugar
2 oz (50 g) butter

1. Butter a 6-inch (15 cm) square tin.

2. Put all ingredients into a pan and stir over a low heat until sugar dissolves.

3. Bring to boil. Cover pan. Boil for 2 minutes. Uncover.

4. Continue to boil fairly gently, without stirring, for about 8 to 10 minutes, or until a little of the mixture forms hard, brittle threads when dropped into a cup of cold water.

5. Pour into prepared tin then using a buttered knife, mark into squares or bars when almost set.

6. Break up when hard and wrap in cling film or clear cellophane.

# Honeycomb

***Makes about 1 lb or 450 g***

*4 oz (125 g) golden syrup*
*4 oz (125 g) clear honey*
*12 oz (350 g) granulated*
  *sugar*
*2 oz (50 g) butter*
*1 tsp vinegar*
*4 tblsp water*
*2 level tsp bicarbonate*
  *of soda*

Another old-fashioned favourite, beloved by people of all ages.

1. Put all ingredients, except bicarbonate of soda, into a large pan.

2. Make as Traditional Toffee (page 59). Remove from heat and stir in bicarbonate of soda. (Mixture will foam up in pan.)

3. Pour into an 8-inch (20 cm) buttered tin and break up when set. Make and eat as soon as possible as Honeycomb quickly becomes sticky.

# Peanut Brittle

*Makes about 1¼ lb or 575 g*

*oz (25 g) butter*
*lb (450 g) granulated
sugar*
*rounded tblsp golden
syrup*
*oz (175 g) unsalted
peanuts, coarsely
chopped*

1. Butter an 8-inch (20 cm) square tin.

2. Put butter, sugar and syrup into a saucepan and stir over low heat until sugar dissolves.

3. Bring to boil. Cover pan. Boil for 2 minutes. Uncover.

4. Continue to boil fairly gently, without stirring, for about 8 to 10 minutes, or until a little of the mixture forms hard, brittle threads when dropped into a cup of cold water.

5. Stir in nuts, then pour into prepared tin.

6. Leave until set, then break up into irregular-shaped pieces with a small hammer. Store in an airtight container.

# Praline

***Makes about 6 oz or 175 g***

*4 oz (125 g) caster sugar*
*2 tblsp water*
*4 oz (125 g) unblanched*
*almonds*

When finely crushed, Praline makes a wonderful addition
homemade ice cream, and it can be used as a decoration for cak
and sundaes. Although classed as a sweet, it is rarely eaten as suc
Once crushed, it should be stored in an airtight tin as dampne
will make it sticky.

1. Put sugar and water into a heavy-based pan and stir over a lo
heat until sugar melts.

2. Mix in almonds and continue to cook until mixture turns a dee
gold, stirring from time to time.

3. Turn out into a buttered dish and leave until firm and set.

4. Break up with a hammer, put on to an oiled work-top and crus
finely with a rolling pin.

5. Transfer to an airtight container and use as required.

# TURKISH DELIGHT

I think it is almost impossible to copy commercially-made Turkish Delight and fruit jellies exactly, but this short section of recipes works satisfactorily and, as yet, I've had no complaints! The recipes do not demand costly ingredients, are all gelatine-based (I used Davis), with the addition of sugar, water, flavourings and colourings. Smothered in icing sugar and put into a carton lined with foil, or cellophane paper, non-stick parchment paper, or cling film, the Turkish Delight would make a welcome gift at any time of year, while the fruit jellies, crisply coated with granulated sugar, are quite delicious and will be enjoyed by both grown-ups and children alike.

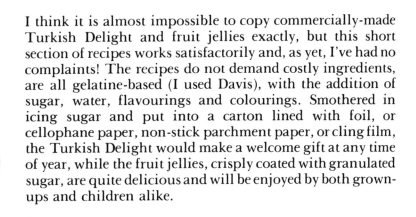

# Rose Turkish Delight

***Makes about 1¼ lb or 575 g***

½ pt (275 ml) hot water
1 oz (25 g) powdered
  gelatine
1 lb (450 g) granulated
  sugar
½ level tsp citric acid
  (available from chemists)
1 tsp rose essence
A few drops of rose pink
  colouring
2 oz (50 g) icing sugar, sifted

Very subtle. A typical middle-eastern sweetmeat.

**1.** Put water into a large saucepan. Shower gelatine on top.

**2.** Stir over a lowish heat until melted. Add sugar and citric acid. Continue to heat until sugar dissolves completely and liquid is clear.

**3.** Raise heat slightly and boil steadily for 20 minutes. Do not stir.

**4.** Add rose essence to mixture, then tint a light pink with the food colouring.

**5.** Pour into an oiled shallow round or square dish – I used an 8-inch (20 cm) round glass baking dish – and leave to stand until cold.

**6.** Put into the refrigerator and leave to stand overnight or for a minimum of 12 hours.

**7.** Tip icing sugar on to a piece of foil.

**8.** Loosen edges of Turkish Delight by running round a knife dipped in hot water.

**9.** To loosen base, stand dish for about 30 seconds in sink containing about 2 inches (5 cm) hot water.

**10.** Using fingers, literally pull Turkish Delight out of dish and turn it on to the icing sugar.

**11.** Cut into 1-inch (2½ cm) squares with scissors, then roll thoroughly in icing sugar so that each piece is heavily coated.

**12.** Transfer, with any spare icing sugar, to a tin with a well-fitting lid.

*Makes about 1¼ lb or 575 g* **Vanilla Turkish Delight**
Make exactly as Rose Turkish Delight but add 1 level teaspoon vanilla essence instead of rose. Leave uncoloured.

*Makes about 1¼ lb or 575 g*

**Peppermint Turkish Delight**
Make exactly as Rose Turkish Delight but add 1 level teaspoon peppermint essence instead of the rose. Tint a pale green with food colouring.

*Makes about 1¼ lb or 575 g*

**Pistachio Turkish Delight**
Make exactly as Rose Turkish Delight but add 1 level teaspoon pistachio essence instead of the rose. Tint deepish green with food colouring.

# Fruit Flavoured Jellies

*Makes about 1¼ lb or 575 g*

½ pt (275 ml) hot water
1 oz (25 g) powdered
   gelatine
1 lb (450 g) granulated
   sugar
½ level tsp citric acid
   (available from chemists)
1 tsp rose essence
A few drops of rose pink
   colouring
3 oz (75 g) granulated sugar

*Makes about 1¼ lb or 575 g*

These are made in exactly the same way as the Rose Turkish Delight on pages 72–73, but are finished differently.

1. Using your fingers, pull the loosened jelly mixture on to a piece of foil covered with 3 oz (75 g) granulated sugar.

2. Cut into 1-inch (2½ cm) squares.

3. Roll in the sugar so that all sides are completely covered.

4. Put on to a plate and leave for about 8 hours to dry.

5. Put into an airtight container to store.

## Lemon Jellies

Make exactly as Rose Turkish Delight but add 1 level teaspoon lemon essence instead of the rose. Tint pale yellow with food colouring. Cut up and toss in granulated sugar.

75

| | |
|---|---|
| *Makes 1¼ lb or 575 g* | **Strawberry Jellies**<br>Make exactly as Lemon Jellies, using strawberry essence and colouring mixture deep pink. |
| *Makes 1¼ lb or 575 g* | **Pineapple Jellies**<br>Make exactly as Lemon Jellies, using pineapple essence and colouring mixture pale yellow. |
| *Makes 1¼ lb or 575 g* | **Raspberry Jellies**<br>Make exactly as Lemon Jellies, using raspberry essence and colouring mixture a deepish red. |
| *Makes 1¼ lb or 575 g* | **Assorted Shaped Jellies**<br>Instead of cutting into squares, cut into strips, triangles or diamonds. For round jellies, cut out with a small biscuit cutter dipped in sugar. |
| *Makes 1¼ lb or 575 g* | **Apple Juice Jellies**<br>Make exactly as Lemon Jellies, but use ½ pt (275 ml) hot apple juice instead of water. |

# COCONUT ICE

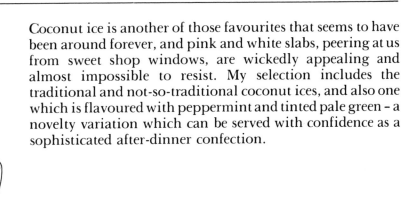

Coconut ice is another of those favourites that seems to have been around forever, and pink and white slabs, peering at us from sweet shop windows, are wickedly appealing and almost impossible to resist. My selection includes the traditional and not-so-traditional coconut ices, and also one which is flavoured with peppermint and tinted pale green – a novelty variation which can be served with confidence as a sophisticated after-dinner confection.

# Coconut Ice with Gelatine

*Makes about 1¼ lb or 575 g*

¼ pt (150 ml) milk
1 lb (450 g) caster sugar
1 tsp vanilla essence
1 level tsp gelatine
4 oz (125 g) desiccated
  coconut
Red food colouring

**1.** Well butter a 6-inch (15 cm) square tin.

**2.** Put milk and sugar into a pan and stir over low heat until sugar dissolves.

**3.** Bring to boil, stirring. Cover pan. Boil for 2 minutes. Uncover.

**4.** Boil steadily for about 20 to 30 minutes, stirring occasionally, until a little of the mixture forms a soft but pliable ball when dropped into a cup of cold water. Stir in vanilla essence.

**5.** Sprinkle gelatine over the top, then cool down to lukewarm.

**6.** Add coconut, then beat until thick and creamy. Spread half into prepared tin.

**7.** Colour remaining coconut ice pale pink with food colouring, then spread quickly over portion in tin.

**8.** Cut into squares when set. Store in an airtight tin.

# Marshmallow Coconut Ice

*Makes about 1¼ lb or 575 g*

1 lb (450 g) granulated
  sugar
¼ pt (150 ml) water
4 oz (125 g) desiccated
  coconut
2 oz (50 g) white
  marshmallows
2 oz (50 g) pink
  marshmallows

1. Well butter a 6-inch (15 cm) square tin.

2. Put sugar and water into a pan and heat slowly, stirring, until sugar dissolves.

3. Increase heat and boil rapidly for 5 minutes only.

4. Stir in coconut, then divide mixture into 2 equal portions.

5. Add white marshmallows to one portion and pink to the other.

6. Beat white portion until thick, creamy and grainy in texture. Spread into tin. Repeat with pink portion and spread over white.

7. Leave until firm and set, then cut into squares. Store in an airtight tin.

# Traditional Coconut Ice

***Makes about 1¼ lb or 575 g***

*4 tblsp milk*
*4 tblsp water*
*1 lb (450 g) granulated*
*sugar*
*4 oz (125 g) desiccated*
*coconut*
*1 tsp vanilla essence*
*Red food colouring*

1. Well butter a 6-inch (15 cm) square tin.

2. Put milk, water and sugar into a saucepan and stir over a low heat until sugar melts.

3. Bring to boil. Cover. Boil for 2 minutes. Uncover.

4. Boil steadily for about 10 to 15 minutes, stirring occasionally, until a little of the mixture forms a soft but pliable ball when dropped into a cup of cold water.

5. Add coconut and vanilla essence. Cool to lukewarm. Beat until thick, creamy and grainy in texture.

6. Spread half into prepare tin. Quickly colour remainder pink with food colouring then spread over first half.

7. Leave until set then cut into squares. Store in an airtight tin.

*Makes about 1¼ lb or 575 g*

**Traditional Peppermint Coconut Ice**

Make exactly as Traditional Coconut Ice but use peppermint essence instead of vanilla and colour half the mixture pale green with food colouring.

# Condensed Milk Coconut Ice

*Makes about 1¼ lb or 575 g*

1 small can sweetened
   condensed milk
9 oz (250 g) icing sugar,
   sifted
1 tsp vanilla essence
6 oz (175 g) desiccated
   coconut
Red food colouring

1. Put condensed milk, sugar and essence into a bowl.

2. Work in the coconut to produce a very stiff mixture.

3. Divide in half and knead a little food colouring into one portion so that it turns pale pink.

4. Shape both pieces into 2 equal-sized bars and press both together.

5. Put on to a plate sprinkled with icing sugar and leave until firm. Cut up into slices. Store in an airtight tin.

# SWEET ASSORTMENT

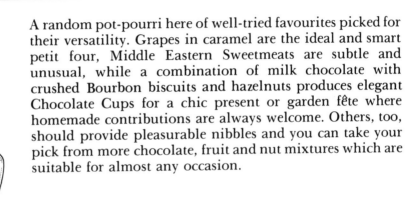

A random pot-pourri here of well-tried favourites picked for their versatility. Grapes in caramel are the ideal and smart petit four, Middle Eastern Sweetmeats are subtle and unusual, while a combination of milk chocolate with crushed Bourbon biscuits and hazelnuts produces elegant Chocolate Cups for a chic present or garden fête where homemade contributions are always welcome. Others, too, should provide pleasurable nibbles and you can take your pick from more chocolate, fruit and nut mixtures which are suitable for almost any occasion.

# Peanut Chocolate Clusters

*Makes 12*

A very easy sweetmeat with an expensive, adult, appeal.

*1 bar (3½ oz or 100 g) plain dessert chocolate*
*1 oz (25 g) butter*
*1 tsp vanilla essence*
*2 oz (50 g) peanuts, coarsely chopped*

**1.** Break up chocolate and put, with butter, into a basin standing over a pan of hot water. Leave until melted, stirring once or twice.

**2.** Mix in essence and nuts.

**3.** Spoon into paper cases and leave until firm before eating.

*Makes 12*

**Walnut Chocolate Clusters**
Make as Peanut Chocolate Clusters but use 2 oz (50 g) chopped walnuts instead of peanuts.

# Apricot Choc Bites

***Makes 20***

4 oz (125 g) dried apricots
Boiling water
1 bar (3½ oz or 100 g) plain
  chocolate
4 oz (125 g) brown
  breadcrumbs
1 or 2 tblsp concentrated
  orange squash or orange
  liqueur
About 1 oz (25 g) icing
  sugar, sifted

Exquisitely-flavoured and delicious with coffee at the end of a
meal.

**1.** Soak apricots in the boiling water for 15 minutes. Drain, then
rinse under cold water.

**2.** Cut into tiny pieces with kitchen scissors.

**3.** Break up chocolate and melt in a basin standing over a pan of
hot water.

**4.** Stir in apricots, breadcrumbs and enough orange squash or
liqueur to make a stiffish mixture.

**5.** Shape into 20 rocky mounds and roll in icing sugar. Refrigerate
for 4 hours before serving.

# Walnut and Violet Petit Fours

***Makes 18***

8 oz (225 g) *icing sugar*
1 oz (25 g) *walnuts, finely crushed in blender or food processor*
½ tsp *finely grated lemon peel*
5 tsp *lemon juice*
4 tsp *clear honey*
1 tsp *vanilla essence*
½ oz (15 g) *crystallised violet petals*

Simple to make, and a perfect end to a special meal.

1. Sift icing sugar into a bowl. Toss in walnuts and lemon peel.

2. Mix to a stiff paste with lemon juice, honey and vanilla essence.

3. Shape into 18 balls, drop into paper cases and put a violet petal on top of each.

# Middle Eastern Sweetmeats

*Makes about 1½ lb or 675 g*

8 oz (225 g) granulated
   sugar
¼ pt (150 ml) water
4 oz (125 g) butter
5 oz (150 g) semolina
2 oz (50 g) raisins
2 level tsp finely grated
   orange peel
2 oz (50 g) ground almonds
½ tsp almond essence

1. Oil or butter an 8-inch (20 cm) square tin.

2. Put sugar and water into a pan and stir over a low heat until sugar dissolves.

3. Bring to boil, cover pan and boil for 2 minutes. Uncover. Boil for a further 3 minutes. Remove from heat.

4. In a separate pan, melt butter then stir in semolina and lightly brown over a medium heat. Mix in raisins, orange peel and almonds.

5. Work in sugar and water syrup, then add essence. Cook, stirring, until mixture gently bubbles and thickens. Simmer for 10 minutes.

6. Pour into tin and leave until cold. Mark into squares and cut up when cold.

# Chocolate Cups

***Makes 12***

4 oz (125 g) milk chocolate
2 oz (50 g) Bourbon
   biscuits, fairly finely
   crushed
12 hazelnuts

A sophisticated combination of ingredients which makes an outstanding chocolate confection for after-dinner eating.

1. Break up chocolate and put into a basin standing over a pan of hot water. Leave until melted, stirring once or twice.

2. Mix in crushed biscuits, then spoon mixture into 12 sweet paper cases.

3. Top each with a hazelnut and refrigerate until firm.

# Caramel Grapes

*Makes about 1½ lb or 675 g*

*1 lb (450 g) mixture of green
and black grapes*
*1 lb (450 g) caster sugar*
*½ pt (275 ml) water*
*1 tsp vinegar*

The ideal petit four.

1. Wash and dry grapes, then cut into pairs with scissors.

2. Put rest of ingredients into a saucepan and stir over a low heat until sugar dissolves.

3. Bring to boil and boil fairly briskly for about 8 minutes or until mixture turns light gold and forms hard, brittle threads when a little is dropped into a cup of cold water.

4. Balancing stalks of grapes through prongs of a fork, dip quickly into caramel to coat.

5. Put on to a piece of oiled greaseproof paper or foil and leave until set. Drop into paper cases. Make and eat on the same day.

# Juicy Fruity Munchies

**Makes 30**

3 heaped tblsp desiccated
  coconut
4 oz (125 g) currants
4 oz (125 g) seedless raisins
4 oz (125 g) sultanas
4 oz (125 g) brazil nuts

A healthy, juicy sweetmeat for children and adults alike.

1. Tip coconut on to a piece of greaseproof paper or foil.

2. Mince currants, raisins, sultanas and nuts.

3. Draw fruit and nut mixture together, then roll into 30 balls.

4. Toss in coconut then drop into paper cases. Chill in the refrigerator until firm.

# Peppermint Chews

**Makes 12 oz or 350 g**

*oz (25 g) butter*
*level tblsp caster sugar*
*level tblsp golden syrup*
*or clear honey*
*tsp peppermint essence*
*½ oz (100 g) dried milk*
*powder (low fat instant)*
*sifted icing sugar*

1. Put butter, sugar, syrup or honey and peppermint essence into a pan.

2. Stir over a low heat until butter melts.

3. Bring to boil and boil briskly for 2 minutes only, or until a little of the mixture forms a soft ball when dropped into a cup of cold water.

4. Remove from heat, stir in milk powder and spoon out on to a plate.

5. When mixture is lukewarm, shape into medium-sized marbles and toss in icing sugar. Store in an airtight tin.

# ACKNOWLEDGEMENTS

Cadbury Schweppes Ltd

Davis Gelatine

Gayles Honey

Suchard Ltd

Wheelbarrow Butter

92

# INDEX